MAKING PEACE WITH YOUR PAST: A 12 STEP GUIDE TO A PEACEFULLY PRODUCTIVE LIFE

by *FELDON BONNER II*

(Foreword by Ivan Sanchez)

POWERHOUSE MINISTRY PUBLISHING, PUBLICATIONS, & PRODUCTIONS, INC., LLC
© 2020 Feldon Bonner II

ISBN (eBook): 978-1-7354921-0-0
ISBN (Paperback): 978-7354921-1-7

Cover design by: Feldon Bonner II (Cover Creator) Photos of Feldon Bonner II and Ivan Sanchez (provided with permission) by: POWERHOUSE PUBLISHING, PUBLICATIONS, & PRODUCTIONS, INC., LLC

Printed in the United States of America

DEDICATION

To God, I humbly thank You, for being Who You are, and doing all that You do (especially, for saving me, and equipping me with everything that pertains to life and godliness)...

To my incredibly loving parents, Feldon Bonner and Willie Mae Hazley Bonner (" Lady Bonner"), I will always be forever indebted unto the Lord, our God, for all that He poured through you both into the spirit of my being...

To my loving wife, Rita M. Bonner (" my Only Everything"), who is the Agent of the Grace, Mercy, and Love of God within my life... May the Lord our God perpetually-permeate through you and continually prosper everything that you do, in the name of Jesus Christ...

To my phenomenal son, Cordadrian Travion Davis, may the Lord's Countenance forever-flow through you, abundantly blessing the lives of everyone within your direct (and indirect) sphere of influence, in the name of Jesus Christ, our Lord and Savior...

To Ashley, Jerry, Jason, Auroya, and Amorie, you are each "jewels" in the crown of God, and "living stones" who are unique in all the world... May the Light of Jesus Christ continue to shine through all of you, for you are fearfully and wonderfully "fashioned" in the likeness of the Chief Cornerstone (Jesus Christ), by" The Jewelry Designer", God Himself.

To James Dixon, Sr. (" only God"); and to all of my family, friends, loved ones, and to everyone who has enriched my Life Experience, pursuant to the dynamics of life, with all of its blessings (and lessons learned), therein. Thank you all.

"... Life *speaks*... The question is: What is your life *saying*?"

Master Feldon Bonner II

CONTENTS

MAKING PEACE WITH YOUR PAST: A 12 STEP GUIDE TO A PEACEFULLY PRODUCTIVE LIFE

By Feldon Bonner II

(Foreword by Ivan Sanchez)

PREFACE: "PEACE (AT ANY COST)"

We all know what it's like to desire "more from our lives", no matter what our present situation may look like.

Pursuant to wanting "more from life", is the crossroad or crisis of defining whether our "more from life" is based upon "quantity", "quality", or somewhere in between "quantity" and "quality".

Rooted and grounded within this personal evaluation, examination, and determination, is the reality that whether we prefer "quantity" or "quality", in both cases, there is no substitute for "peace". In any event, when it comes to wanting "more from life", the absence of peace, nullifies the "substance" of either "quantity" or "quality".

Ultimately, we come to the conclusion that "peace" must be defined, established, internalized, obtained, maintained, and sustained (at any cost).

Fulfillment, purpose, significance, resilience, success, and perpetual transition into greatness, is purchased, ransomed, and redeemed, by the realized true experience of an attained-peace.

The soul-quenching answer to life, is articulated through the quest for mastering the process of making peace with your past.

The reconciling-process may be painful, but the end-result is "rest" for the weary soul, and to the one who is on such a spiritual-journey, there is an inner cry for "peace (at any cost)"…

ABOUT THE AUTHOR

FELDON BONNER II is a Christian Minister, Civil Rights Advocate, Entrepreneur, Songwriter, Producer, and Motivational Speaker, who addresses multi-ethnic audiences on the faith-based "keys" to breaking self-sabotaging/ erroneous-thinking patterns, overcoming self (and systematically)-imposed obstacles, and systemic oppressive cycles.

He is the Founder and Executive Director of **POWERHOUSE MINISTRY**, which is a 501(c)(3) nonprofit organization.

He is also the Founder and Executive Director of **POWERHOUSE PUBLISHING, PUBLICATIONS, & PRODUCTIONS, INC. LLC., POWERHOUSE MINISTRY TELEVISION,** and **POWERHOUSE RECOVERY RADIO.**

He has facilitated multi-faceted cognitive mentor programs, within various communities, via **POWERHOUSE COMMUNITY DEVELOPMENT CORPORATION**, while also engaging in faith-based cognitive classes within several prison units, state jails, and recovery-ready treatment centers.

FOREWORD

by *Ivan Sanchez*

President of Houston Millennials; Real Estate Investor at Sanmore Investments; Former U.S. Congressional District 7 Candidate; and Commercial Lender at Gold Quest Group, LLC

Initially, upon reading "*Making Peace With Your Past: A 12 Step Guide To A Peacefully Productive Life*", the first thing that you inescapably discover is that this book is a "call to action". Page-by-page, you are bombarded with mandates to examine yourself, and to actually utillze the tools that are before you (and within you), in order to begin to make peace in every area of your life that you choose to apply these truths and principles towards.

"*Making Peace With Your Past*" observes that History, Mankind, and Society (as we know it) is affected by perpetual dysfunction, and dysfunction is at the core essence and foundation of an inexhaustible list of life challenging circumstances and situations, which "surface" as: racism, inequity, inequality, injustices, political factions, religious seditions, all forms of "abuse", and systemic oppression (all of these manifestations can be traced back to some degree, form, or measure of dysfunctionalism. We all have our dysfunctional beginning (no matter what our social or economic status may be, dysfunction still fuels our lives and our choices), until we make peace with the dysfunction of our past. We often interact with one another through filters and paradigms of generational harm, injury, and hurt (where little, if any, peace whatsoever has been made from the past), and it is from this place of cultural and systematic dysfunction, that our stories individually pick up, as we enter (and/ or as we are "birthed" onto life's stage, in the spotlight of our dysfunction...

... As a disoriented teenager, I was fending for myself and living a so-called "street life". At that season, part of my challenges were derived from me grieving the death of my "Superwoman"-my Mother. My life was in a dysfunctional upheaval, still, I somehow determined that schoolwork might be my clearest means towards "success". I recall making intentional decisions to take charge of my destiny, and I unconsciously started the "pursuit" of my own "happiness". Through life's disappointments, adversity, struggles, naysayers, "broke" bank accounts, and life lessons, I ultimately rejected the narrative that I was "a troubled and directionless youth", and replaced that narrative with my own: I am a young "man of integrity and influence" I exchanged my "broke" past of empty bank accounts, for a family-owned company that has lent over $ 500 million dollars to community development investors. Overcoming the adversity that I faced from the past, also fueled my desire to serve others, and to help them to improve their lives. We, as a people, are not predestined to misery, failure, and dysfunction. I represent a new generation of leadership. I refuse to accept the status quo policies that adversely-affect our disadvantaged and vulnerable communities. The challenges that I faced from being a deprived, low socioeconomic teenager, to becoming an empowered Congressional Laison, allowed me to evolve, grow and adapt, and to become a mediator of change, but more importantly, it gave me the inspiration to further help the underprivileged, as one who has walked in those very shoes myself. My endeavor, in part, is to continue to make changes and achievements, because I see the endless possibilities for my life (and for the lives of the people who constitute the world around me)."

To any struggling young person who is reading this book: "Rise Up, Dust Yourself Off, and Find Your Passion! I want you to know that if I could do it, truly, you can do it as well! Do the best that you can, with what you can, while you can, but do it passionately, tirelessly, and vigorously." It is never too late to reinvent yourself! Look in the mirror; that's your only "competition". Today, you can begin "Making Peace With Your Past"."

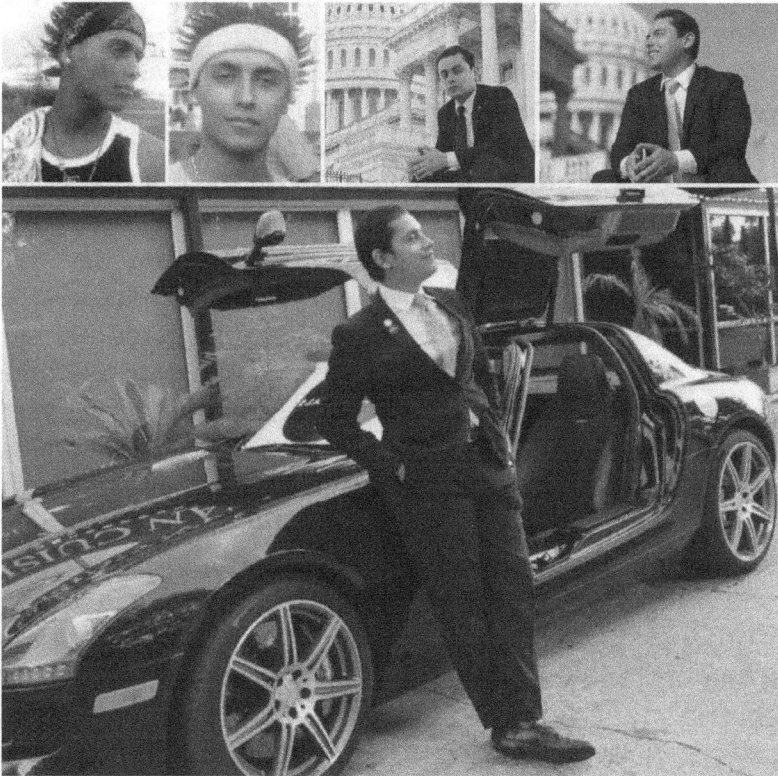

YOU NEED TO READ THIS BOOK!

You may be in need of making peace with your past, from life situations that are from the affects of addiction within your life (whether it was your own addiction or someone else's addictive cycle);

You may be in need of making peace with your past, involving some form of a toxic or abusive relationship;

You may be in need of making peace with your past, in reference to the death of someone close to you;

You may be in need of making peace with an unexpected divorce, an investment that did not pan out as you had planned, or a painful past from unforeseen circumstances and situations.

Making peace with your past is necessitated for faith-building and capacity-building, for daily resiliency, for spiritual sustainability and for enduring-success.

This book is an atrium to problem-solving, and it will definitely prove to be helpful, in the process of making peace with your past.

CURRICULUM COVENANT

INTRODUCTION: THE BIBLICAL DEFINITION OF A "PEACEMAKER"

THE BLESSING OF "MAKING PEACE WITH YOUR PAST"

PREPARATION FOR THE PROCESS OF MAKING PEACE"

CURRICULUM COVENANT

"For where two or three are gathered together in my name, there am I in the midst of them." (Matt. 18: 18)

✓ I agree that I need God in order to make peace with my past.

✓ I agree that attendance to all sessions is my top priority.

✓ I agree to complete all assignments.

✓ I agree to do my part in creating an atmosphere of trust within the group.

✓ I agree to be honest with myself and others, and to support the members of the support group.

✓ I agree to be confronted by others, in love, in order to make peace with my past, and in order to grow.

Signed _____

Date _____

This course offers a faith-based, facilitator-directed, self-help peer group, and it does not offer any form of professional and/ or clinical therapy.

INTRODUCTION: THE BIBLICAL DEFINITION OF A "PEACEMAKER"

"Blessed are the ***PEACEMAKERS*** for they shall be called the children of God." [Matthew 5: 9]

In the Greek text, the word "***Peacemaker***" is translated from the Greek word eirenopoios (Greek #1518), which is derived from a combination of several Greek words:

eirene (Greek #1515-1517)-to join; to make one; set at one again; unite; harmonize; salutary; rest; prosperity; quietness; make peace.

poieo (Greek #4160)-to make or do; avenge; appoint; agree; abide; band together for a common cause; commit or commission; content; contend; deal; execute; hold; keep; lay (in) wait; lighten the ship; none of these things move me; ordain; perform; a service or duty; provide a service or duty; in service or duty; to have a purpose; work.

prasso (Greek #4238)-" practice"; perform repeatedly or habitually; a single, yet, continuing act; accomplish; commit; commission; deeds; use arts or gifts.

"PEACEMAKERS" are:

[1] Those who actively-work to bring about peace and reconciliation, where there is (and/ or has been) hatred and enmity, by sharing Christ's Ministry (the Gospel Message of peace and reconciliation) [2 Cor. 5: 18-19; Eph. 2: 14-16; Col. 1: 20].

[2] Ambassadors/ Representatives, who are commissioned, equipped, and empowered to be sent out, with all authority and power to act and speak for the One Who has sent them [Matt. 28: 18-20; Eph. 2: 14-16; Col. 1: 20].

[3] Those who are delegated authority to solve disputes; erase divisions; reconcile (in) difference(s); eliminate strife; silence tongues; build "right" relationships.

[4] Those who confront, handle, settle, conquer all struggle(s), tension(s), difficulties, opposition(s), pressure(s), rebellion(s), adversity, strife [including crisis management and problem-solving, which are all, various forms of peace-making].

[5] Those who are of the similitude of a peace officer (law enforcement official, security guard, national guard, armed forces officer/ official), who are delegated authority to establish, maintain, and/ or to restore peace and order.

A **peacemaker's commission** (and/ or duty) places them in the middle of conflict, disputes, strife, etc., in order to bring about peace between opposing parties.

Example(s):

[1] An officer responding to a domestic dispute;

[2] Riots being dispersed, controlled, or eliminated; and/
or

[3] Rebellious individuals (or law-breakers) being
brought into captivity.

A "**peacemaker**" knows that conflicts, battles, and/ or bloodshed are sometimes necessitated to make peace. Jesus Christ was a "Peacemaker", Who made/ accomplished peace with God, our Father, by confronting the issue of our rebellious sin, which separated us from God and classified us as enemies of God.

As **peacemakers** (enlisted by/ in Christ), we are commissioned, with delegated authority, to serve God (and to serve others), pursuant to the ministry (service) of reconciliation, no matter what it takes or costs. We must faithfully-serve, using the spiritual weapons that have been entrusted to us.

A "**peacemaker**" conquers the inner struggles; settles the inner conflict, tension, and strife, "for the good", while conquering the bad or evil.

A "**peacemaker**" does not passively-accept trouble, nor do they ignore, flee, nor evade the problem(s), threatening-situation(s), nor compulsive behavior, that violates the peaceful law of the land (or the Law of God).

THE "BLESSING" OF "MAKING PEACE WITH YOUR PAST"

"For all have sinned, and come short of the glory of God." (Romans 3: 23).

There is peacemaking-power in this verse, when you understand that it is all-inclusive, as encompassing and referencing sin, in the form of both our actions and our identity, (which have both been redeemed and reconciled by/ through Christ Jesus)!!

There are two reluctantly-evasive admissions that have the potential to empower and bless you, no matter what your personal background and social status may consist of:

[1] "I need Jesus Christ, because I HAVE messed up" (which pertains to your ACTIONS);

[2] "I need Jesus Christ, because I AM messed up" (which pertains to your IDENTITY).

These two spiritually-empowering confessions can open up the door to self-examination and emancipation. The truth is that we all share a common need to make peace with our past in some manner and/ or area of our life.

This curriculum was designed to lead you through a study of the influences of growing up in a family, community, and/ or environment, where the presence of dysfunction disrupted the development of healthy behaviors and relationships.

This curriculum will provide interactive guidance to assist you in identifying and understanding the present feelings and problems that may be related to your past experiences.

"Making Peace With Your Past" will help you:

1. **Identify** and **understand** present problems and feelings from past experiences;

2. **Identify** ways that the past affects you in the present;

3. **Understand** that other people have experienced similar problems and feelings;

4. **Unlock** buried feelings from the past and experience healing and forgiveness;

5. **Experience** an atmosphere of trust, honesty, and unconditional love;

6. **Identify** and **remove** emotional, psychological, and spiritual barriers to your fellowship with God;

7. **Experience** a true sense of hope and healing.

PEER SUPPORT GROUP

Because this study may guide you to connect with (and/ or to get in touch with) powerful memories or emotions, you may need to study it with a small, caring group of people.

This small support group will come face-to-face with persons who "hurt", yet, who have hope for healing, and who will experience the acceptance, love, and presence of Jesus Christ.

FACE-TO-FACE
SUPPORT GROUP

A. HOW A SUPPORT GROUP WORKS

You are about to meet people, who will become your support group during this study, as you work together to make peace with your past. You are also about to meet "yourself". You are about to experience, first-hand, that there are others who are just like you, who are still dealing with unresolved issues. You will find that God can use your support group to bring about a powerful change in your life, as the following four group dynamics begin to take place.

1. DEVELOPING TRUST

As the climate of trust develops, you may find courage to let others see the real you, which is the first step to getting help. When you begin to let the group see you as you really are, healing can begin.

2. REALIZING THAT "I AM NOT ALONE"

As you hear other persons tell their stories, you will realize that you are not alone. Your story and your pain are unique, but others have similar stories and similar pain. Hearing another person describe pain you have felt, but never verbalized, has a healing effect. Knowing that others hurt, just as you hurt, pulls you out of an isolated world of emotional pain.

3. DISCOVERING FEELINGS AND MEMORIES

As other group members share their pain, their fears, and their emotions, you may recover lost emotions. As you hear someone else tell their story, you may be able to recover memories that were previously hidden.

4. RECEIVING FEEDBACK

Group members can identify areas in which you may have "blind spots". They can help you discover feelings you suppress. They may offer interpretive insights into the incidents you describe and share. God often uses groups to bring healing and peace!

PREPARATION FOR THE PROCESS OF MAKING PEACE

B. KEYS TO GROUP PROGRESS

1. TRUST. Be willing to trust and to build trust.

2. WORK ON YOUR OWN ISSUES. Don't try to solve the other group members' problems. Don't offer quick, opinionated, and simplistic solutions. Listen. Empathize. Share your own feelings. Examine your own feelings.

3. IDENTIFY YOUR FEELINGS. Let yourself feel your own emotions, as other group members tell their stories. Be willing to share your feelings with the group.

Abandonment	**Anger**	**Anxiety**
Fear	**Guilt**	**Loneliness**
Mistrust	**Pain**	**Rejection**
Resentment	**Sadness**	**Shame**

Of course, many other feelings can be experienced. These are some feelings which some members of a dysfunctional family have trouble either feeling or expressing, and these feelings and emotions are most likely to be deeply buried, like land mines, that can be activated when triggered. In a support group, we can begin to deactivate these emotional detonators. We can face our hurts and pain, and by doing so, we can overcome it.

Realize that even while you are in the midst of your own "peers" and in a "peer" support group setting, it is still "normal" to initially have difficulty with expressing (or even identifying) your feelings.

4. LISTEN. Learn to listen to what may be expressed "between the lines". Learn to listen with your emotions, as well as with your ears. What do you feel as you listen to another group member share? What messages are being conveyed "between the lines"?

5. THE WORD OF GOD IS THE EXCLUSIVE AUTHORITY.

The Word of God (the Holy Bible) should be the final and/ or exclusive authority in all discussions.

C. TYPES OF GROUP RESPONSES

As members of your group share (during the sessions), you can encourage them in several ways:

1. SAY, "I SUPPORT YOU": As a group member shares something that is obviously difficult to share, you can encourage that person with the simple words, "I support you". However, put forth an extra effort to guard against allowing "I support you" from becoming a sarcastic cliche within your group."

2. GIVE FEEDBACK: Feedback is not giving answers to questions. It is telling a group member what you have seen and heard, as you have watched and listened. The best part of feedback, is when a person is on the receiving end, and it is best, when we are able to listen carefully. This type of feedback is even better that "corrective criticism", because it has the kinetic potential to truly be transformative and life-changing.

D. FACING YOUR FEARS

1. BREAKING THE CARDINAL RULE OF EVERY DYSFUNCTIONAL FAMILY (THE RULE OR CODE OF SILENCE). Don't talk about the problem. That's family business!" We need help for the pain that we feel, and the only true way to obtain it, is to begin to talk about the things that hurt you (us).

2. **YOU MAY FEEL THAT BEING IN A GROUP MEANS YOU ARE BEING DISLOYAL TO YOUR FAMILY.** The support group is not an agent of attack nor criticism, but, an avenue to emotional and spiritual healing, thus, the things that are shared are not to be deemed as being critical of your family, but simply a means of addressing emotional wounds that are hurting your relationship with (or your memory of) your family members.

3. **YOUR FEAR MAY BE CAUSED BY YOUR DIFFICULTY IN TRUSTING OTHER PEOPLE.** In the past, you may have trusted, and consequently, have been hurt; thus, you may not be sure if you want to trust your support group.

You must be willing to share, in order to grow through the group process, but, that is your decision. You will learn to sense an appropriate level of trust in your support group.

How do you deal with your fear of beginning the support group process?

Admit it.
Face it.
Go to the first support group session. Participate.
Begin making peace with your past...

E. REVIEW OF GROUP ASSUMPTIONS

You will help your support group accomplish its objectives, by remembering and assisting with the following guidelines:

1. Start each session on time.

2. No one is ever forced to say anything in a session, but all are encouraged to share, to move toward growth.

3. Introduce yourself by your real first and last name, as opposed to nicknames, abbreviated references to your name, etc. (this is about "getting real", not being anonymous, it's also an opportunity to redefine who you really are).

4. Whatever is shared in the group is confidential.

5. Attempt to sit in a circle and remove all empty seats.

6. Stay focused on what is being shared; keep any writing or note-taking at a minimum (to deter distractions or noninvolvement).

7. Reread the support group Curriculum Covenant at each session.

STEP 1: DEFINING AND IDENTIFYING DYSFUNCTION AND SELF-ESTEEM DEVELOPMENT

1. DEFINITION AND CHARACTERISTICS OF A DYSFUNCTIONAL FAMILY

DEFINITION OF A DYSFUNCTIONAL FAMILY

Dysfunctional: to be unable to function properly or efficiently; to be imperfect; erroneous; flawed; un-whole; having a void, lack, or deficit in some manner of operation, purpose, ability, capability, order, structure, discipline, development, growth, and strength.

CHARACTERISTICS OF A DYSFUNCTIONAL FAMILY

A **dysfunctional** family:

1. Is closed to the spiritual (and outside) world

2. Fails to provide appropriate nurture for its members

3. Allows counter-productive (and destructive) roles

4. Discourages open talk about obvious problems

5. Limits the expression of emotions/ feelings

6. Enables dysfunction to continue

7. Incubates addictive/ compulsive behavioral patterns in its members

1. A Dysfunctional Family Is Closed To The Spiritual (And "Outside") World

"SPIRITUAL" WORLD

A dysfunctional family is closed to the spiritual world. It closes out the activity of the Holy Spirit. It is closed to the Spirit of God, the Word of God, and the Peace of God. It remains closed to individual (and corporate) spiritual growth. All of Mankind falls under this category of spiritual dysfunction, and thus, we all stand in need of divine intervention, to open up such a spiritually-closed door.

B. "OUTSIDE" WORLD

A dysfunctional family is closed to the outside world. It closes out responsible interaction (commission) with the outside world. It also often shuts out the outside world, because it has something that it doesn't want to get out, and/ or something that it doesn't want the outside world to come into... A dysfunctional family often has a family "secret" (hidden issues), which reject any outside interaction, interference, and influence, that may have the potential of exposing, making peace, bringing settlement, and solving destructive behavioral patterns in its members.

2. A Dysfunctional Family Fails to Provide Appropriate Nurture For its Members

In the plan of God, a family is biblically-designed to create and/ or provide an atmosphere of trust (and a sense of safety) for its members: where they can learn to be nurtured, cherished, cared for, unified, and loved.

In essence, God Himself reveals Himself as the covenant-keeping Triune God (who, is a Divine Being/ Family within Himself: Father, Son, and Holy Spirit). The fundamental characteristic of God Himself, is to love, cherish, care, and nurture, and thus, to love, cherish, care, and nurture should be the fundamental characteristic(s) of the "family" unit of God, pursuant to "humanity" being created in the image of God.

With this much understood, in such a family, *"peacemaking"* (and/ or problem-solving) should be an on-going, daily, and constant process, as relationships are formed, cultivated, and developed.

The class on *"PEACEMAKING 101"* should begin within the family, because within a Biblically-functioning-family, on a daily basis, its members learn, that unresolved issues need to be addressed and resolved (i.e., making peace).

A dysfunctional family primarily does not create and maintain an environment where love, honesty, loyalty, dignity, trust, spiritual growth, and nurturing can take place.

Write down how you relate to this, and be very specific.

3. A Dysfunctional Family Allows Counter-Productive (and Destructive) Roles

There are natural "roles" for each member of every family, which are productive in nature. These roles undergird and strengthen the individual family members, as well as the whole family.

However, in a dysfunctional family, its members develop roles to survive in an emotionally detrimental surrounding of spiritual destitution and deprivation.

Counter-productive (and destructive) roles begin to surface, and a dysfunctional family allows such roles to be assumed and adopted, as **"the Norm"** (or as a normal behavior pattern).

Such **"roles"** may be unconsciously chosen by a family member, or it may be unofficially assigned by the family, without even being aware that this has even taken place.

 A few easily-recognized "roles" in a dysfunctional family are:

"HERO"-Works hard to bring respect to the family name

"SCAPEGOAT"-Usually blamed for family problems

"SURROGATE SPOUSE"-Often a child takes the place of an emotionally absent spouse and becomes a child counselor for a troubled adult parent

"QUIET ONE"-Never gets in the way or causes trouble because this family already has enough problems

Write down how you relate to this, and be very specific.

4. A Dysfunctional Family Discourages Open Talk About Obvious Problems

Everyone has problems, and in all actuality, daily-conflict is a normal part of family life. In a healthy emotional environment, conflict resolution abounds. However, in an unhealthy or dysfunctional environment, open dialogue about situations, circumstances, challenges, and problems are not welcomed, and ultimately, discouraged. This alludes to dysfunction being sustained, in multi-faceted forms, with seemingly, irreparable affects, consequences, or results.

Write down how you relate to this, and be very specific.

5. A Dysfunctional Family Limits the Expression of Emotions/ Feelings

In a dysfunctional family the expression of emotions and feelings are often limited, which restricts its members from being free to express their own individualized/ personalized feelings and emotions.

In a dysfunctional family the emotional instability and imbalance of one member can be emotionally-contagious to the other members, because sometimes the other family members begin to live out their emotions and feelings, based upon the emotions and feeling of the emotionally unstable and imbalanced family member. (Example: Mom is "upset", so the rest of the family is "upset", no matter how "nice " or "pleasant" their day has been).

An "Alpha-Emotionalist" is allowed to be the individual, whose emotions dictates and determines the trajectory of emotions for everyone in the family (directly and indirectly).

Write down how you relate to this, and be very specific.

6. A Dysfunctional Family Enables Dysfunction to Continue

Peacemaking (and/or making peace) is not a trait of a dysfunctional family, because a dysfunctional family is an enabler, and it enables dysfunction, chaos, crisis, disorder, disunity, problems, conflicts, and erroneous thinking patterns (and behavior) to continue, without seeking assistance, help, counseling, and peace-making.

Write down how you relate to this, and be very specific.

7. A Dysfunctional Family Incubates Addictive/ Compulsive Behavioral Patterns in its Members

It is well known that seeds eventually take root, cultivate, grow, and bear fruit. A dysfunctional family actually incubates addictive/ compulsive behavior patterns in the lives of the family members.

The following are a few examples of such Addictive/ Compulsive Behavioral Pattern(s):

a. **Alcoholic**: addicted to alcoholic
b. **Drug Addict**: addicted to drug(s)
c. **Rage-aholic**: pattern of intense outbursts of anger or rage d. **Work Addiction**: absent in the house, yet addicted to work
e. **Sex Addict**: addicted to pornography; endless string of sexual relationships that lack (or avoid) true emotional intimacy; and sex crime (such as indecent exposure, violent sexual abuse, and rape).
f. **Eating Disorder(s)**: compulsively eating too little or too much; "binging" (or gorging themselves with food) and "purging" (forced vomiting or elimination)
g. **Spending/ Gambling Addict**: addicting to spending or gambling compulsively
h. **Religion Addict**: engages in compulsive religious activities, while lacking emotional and spiritual health (outward obedience with inward rebellion).

Write down how you relate to this, and be very specific.

2. EXAMINATION AND EVALUATION: "AM I THE MEMBER OF A DYSFUNCTIONAL FAMILY?"

At this point, we have laid a solid and sound foundation, by establishing the necessary definitions for this curriculum, and therefore, we can now begin the on-going "process" of self-examination and self-evaluation. We will earnestly and honestly initiate this "process", by simply asking and answering one simple question: **"AM I THE MEMBER OF A DYSFUNCTiONAL FAMILY?"**

Please, allow me to help you out; The Answer is: **"YES."**

As we have previously discussed, in a dysfunctional family, shame suffocates self-esteem, and one of self-esteem's greatest enemies is shame. When one family member's behavior causes shame to another family member, it can become difficult for the other family member to develop a high sense of self-esteem. It's difficult to have high self-esteem, when you are feeling shame towards a member of your family (and/ or feeling shame for the behavior of a member of your family). In a dysfunctional family, shame tears down the edifice of self-esteem, and a family member develops a shame-based identity (wherein, shame lies at the root of a person's identity). In a dysfunctional family, a person is ashamed of their father's behavior; their mother's actions; their sibling's conduct. The shame becomes so deeply-rooted, that it embodies who you are, and it goes right down to the core of your inner being. In such cases, a person may attempt to hide their shame by distancing themselves from the embarrassing family member; isolating the family member; reducing interaction or public encounters with the family member; masking themselves in achievements; cover the shame with a façade of self-assurance and self-assertiveness, but the shame is still there, at the foundation of your identity, becoming an self-obstructive obstacle that must be overcome, in order to make peace with your past. As we have looked at these definition(s), characteristics, traits, and activities that are parallel with our own family of origin, we should conclude, **"Yes...I am the member of a dysfunctional family."**

Write down how you relate to this, and be very specific.

3. INFLUENCES OF YOUR "FAMILY OF ORIGIN" UPON THE DEVELOPMENT OF YOUR SELF-ESTEEM

Your "family of origin" is your direct (and/ or indirect) sphere of influence. It influences the edification and development of your self-esteem, and it affirms its family members in the following ways:
1. It acknowledges a family member's feelings.
2. It responds to a family member's feelings.
3. It nurtures a family member's feelings.
4. When appropriate, it affirms a family member's feelings.

Write down how you relate to this, and be very specific.

On the contrary, within a dysfunctional "family of origin", the dysfunctionalism has an adverse affect upon the development of your self-esteem.

Dysfunctional Families Tear Down Self-Esteem...

1. By Teaching Family Members That Their Feelings Are Not Important

A family member's feelings may be ignored or overlooked, as the dysfunctional family simply tries to get from one crisis to the next, so they can survive. In such a time, people may begin to feel unacknowledged and un-affirmed.

Write down how you relate to this, and be very specific.

2. Because Family Members Lose Perspective Of What Is Normal

When no one knows what it means to be a "normal" family, people have to guess what normal is, what normal feels like, and what normal looks like. Normal may become what "other people are" and what "other people do".

Write down how you relate to this, and be very specific.

3. By Failing To Develop A Strategy of Problem-Solving for Relational and Emotional Issues

"Making peace" is related to "problem-solving" for relationships and emotional issues. Life does not have to be consumed by problems. Decisions ultimately appear to be "fatalistic", with little or "no resolution" being offered for challenging or problematic situations.

Write down how you relate to this, and be very specific.

4. By Permitting Unhealthy Survival Roles

Survival roles are the result of substituting who a person really is, and what they should be expected to do, with whoever they feel they need to be, and do, to survive a crisis or critical time.

Write down how you relate to this, and be very specific.

5. By Failing To Nurture One Another

Healthy self-esteem development is stunted, when people do not nurture each other emotionally.

Write down how you relate to this, and be very specific.

6. By Transferring Shame It's hard to have high self-esteem, when you feel ashamed for a member of your family. After you feel this shame for a period of time, you may develop a shame-based identity. This means that a sense of shame lies at the root of your identity. The shame is so deep, that it is a part of who you are. The shame goes to the core of your being. You may hide it with achievements, or cover it with a mask of self-assurance, but the shame is firmly-planted, at the base of your identity.

Write down how you relate to this, and be very specific.

YOUR THOUGHTS: 1. Definition and Characteristics of a Dysfunctional Family

Write down how you relate to this, an be very specific.

YOUR THOUGHTS: 2. Examination and Evaluation: "Am I the Member of a Dysfunctional Family?"

Write down how you relate to this, and be very specific.

YOUR THOUGHTS: 3. Influences of your Family of Origin upon the Development of Your Self-Esteem

Write down how you relate to this, and be very specific.

YOUR THOUGHTS: 4. Identifying Ways to Get in Touch With Your Feelings

Write down how you relate to this, and be very specific.

YOUR THOUGHTS: 5. Losing Self-Esteem in a Dysfunctional Family: Connection Between Your Dysfunctional Family's Influence and the Development of Low Self-Esteem

Write down how you relate to this, and be very specific.

YOUR THOUGHTS: 6. Finding Self-Esteem in Christ

Write down how you relate to this, and be very specific.

A.   I Can't

B. God Can

C. I Am Going To Let Him

D. (See STEP 11: THE EMPOWERMENT OF "I CAN")

Affirmation and Meditation: "I accept God's Love for me."

"There is therefore now no condemnation to them which are in Christ Jesus." (Romans 8:1)

IDENTIFYING WAYS TO GET IN TOUCH WITH YOUR FEELINGS

We all have feelings. We all express our feelings, one way or another. However, many of us tend to have difficulty, when it comes to actually identifying what we are truly feeling. In other words, we can clearly feel a certain way, but we may not be able to identify what it is that we are truly feeling. Do you have trouble identifying your feelings?"

A.   Why do some of us have trouble identifying feelings?

1. You may have learned to live out someone else's feelings, in stead of our own.
2. Your family may have discouraged or suppressed the expression of feelings.
3. You may have been taught that certain feelings were ok, while other feelings were not ok, should not exist within you, nor should be expressed, vocalized, nor discussed openly.
4. You may be a victim of chronic-shock syndrome.

Write down how you relate to this, and be very specific.

Chronic-Shock Syndrome is when you have experienced emotional feelings that are so intense, that your emotional system shuts down, while being locked in the feelings of the moment.

B. Why do you need to share your feelings? Feelings were created to be expressed. Feelings that are held inside, will find a way out. You can share your feelings, or you can wait for them to come out by some other means. Feelings have a tendency to express themselves in unplanned ways, when they are being denied or held inside, such as: Acting Out-behavior based on hidden feelings Illness-can result from internalized or withheld feelings.

C. You May Be Using Defensive Methods To Avoid or Stay Out of Touch with Your Feelings

People who have operated on emotional overload, often learn defensive methods of keeping their distance from their feelings, or blocking out or denying their feelings.

Intellectualizing. Trying to keep thoughts and conversation on rational things and intellectual matters, rather than on feelings and emotions.

Minimizing. Downplaying your feelings, hurts, pain, and emotions.
Denial. Denying and/ or ignoring any feeling or emotion exists.

Isolating. When emotions and feelings surface, you retreat to a safe zone, where you have control or you create an imaginary world, where these emotions do not affect or have an influence on you.

Swallowing a Feeling. You find ways to hold back or to internalize what you are feeling.

Taking Care of Others. You focus on others, or on someone else's feelings or needs, instead of your own. You're eager to help someone else to solve their problem, but you are evasive about addressing your own problem. You empathize with the feelings of others, but you desensitize your own feelings and emotions.

These are just a few methods that people often use to avoid their feelings.

"Do you use any of these methods or techniques to stay out of touch with your feelings?"

Write out some of your own personal methods or techniques that you utilize to stay out of touch with your feelings:

5. LOSING SELF-ESTEEM IN A DYSFUNCTIONAL FAMILY: CONNECTION BETWEEN YOUR DYSFUNCTIONAL FAMILY'S INFLUENCE AND THE DEVELOPMENT OF LOW SELF-ESTEEM

Both a Functional Family and a Dysfunctional Family are is a sphere of influence upon the development of self-esteem of its family members.

Ultimately a Functional Family's influence builds up self-esteem, while a Dysfunctional Family's influence tears down self-esteem.

Here are few ways that a dysfunctional family's influence tears down self-esteem, and conclusively, how a functional family builds up self-esteem.

REMINDER: A DYSFUNCTIONAL FAMILY'S INFLUENCE "TEARS DOWN" SELF-ESTEEM:

1. BY TEACHING ITS MEMBERS THAT THEIR FEELINGS ARE NOT IMPORTANT

Most Dysfunctional families are crisis-oriented, wherein, there is a pattern of crisis after crisis, and there is never an opportunity provided to process emotions or feelings during crisis. Feelings are suppressed and not encouraged to be discussed nor expressed. Feelings are not important, only survival from crisis.

Write down how you relate to this, and be very specific.

2. BECAUSE ITS MEMBERS LOSE PERSPECTIVE ON WHAT IS "NORMAL"

In a dysfunctional family, its members have to guess at what "normal" is. They basically have little idea of what a "normal" functioning family is like.

Write down how you relate to this, and be very specific.

3. BY FAILING TO DEVELOP A STRATEGY OF PROBLEM-SOLVING FOR RELATIONAL AND EMOTIONAL ISSUES

In a dysfunctional family, problem-solving methods, practices, strategies or tools are neglected or non-existent, which alludes to an acceptance of a perpetual problematic state of "I will always have this problem", "I will always be like this", "I cannot do anything to change", "Life will always be just like this for me", "There is no solution or answer to this situation or problem."

Write down how you relate to this, and be very specific.

4. BY PERMITTING UNHEALTHY SURVIVAL ROLES

In a healthy atmosphere, individuals are free to become who they are intended, and in an unhealthy family atmosphere of influence, uniqueness is discouraged, and survival roles are imposed or substituted for who the person is intended to become.

Write down how you relate to this, and be very specific.

5. BY FAILING TO NUTURE ONE ANOTHER

Members develop healthy self-esteem as they are nurtured in an environment of love. In an atmosphere that is largely absent of emotional nurture, the healthy self-esteem that is possible in an individual may be thwarted.

Write down how you relate to this, and be very specific.

REMINDER: A FUNCTIONAL FAMILY'S INFLUENCE BUILDS UP SELF-ESTEEM:

1. BY ACKNOWLEDGING FAMILY MEMBERS' FEELINGS

2. BY RESPONDING TO FAMILY MEMBERS' FEELINGS

3. BY AFFIRMING FAMILY MEMBERS' FEELINGS

4. BY NURTURING FAMILY MEMBERS'S FEELINGS

5. BY RECOGNIZING OUR NEED FOR GOD/ CHRIST DO MEET OUR EMOTIONAL ESTEEM NEEDS

6. FINDING SELF-ESTEEM IN CHRIST

A.I CAN'T

B. GOD CAN

C. I AM GOING TO LET HIM

D. (See STEP 11: THE EMPOWERMENT OF "I CAN")

AFFIRMATION AND SCRIPTURAL MEDITATION: "I accept God's Love for me."

"There is therefore now no condemnation to them which are in Christ Jesus." (Romans 8:1)

Write down how you relate to this, and be very specific.

STEP 2: DEFINING AND DISCERNING COMPULSIVE BEHAVIOR

STEP 2: DEFINING AND DISCERNING COMPULSIVE BEHAVIOR

Compulsive Behavior is involves a pattern of doing the same thing, primarily, the same way, repetitiously and ritualistically. It often has hidden causes that are not easily detected and/ or discoverable without intensified self-examination and evaluation. Such behavior has a driving force that is extremely challenging to confront and overcome, because it is driven by an inexhaustible inner force.

Compulsive behavior eats at an individual and can ultimately, consume a person, to the extent of expending all of a person's energy, draining even the person's will power to put forth an effort to overcome their own compulsion(s).

Furthermore, compulsive behavior is, within itself, its own defense mechanism to avoid or evade solutions, answers, and key elements or tools to overcome ingrained, learned, suppressed emotions, feelings, and erroneous paradigms, ultimately combating, denying, and refusing to even allow probes or questions that could allude to resolution to dysfunction.

Dangerously, yet, revelatory, compulsive behavior also possesses the ability to also reproduce itself, by breeding or regenerating multi-faceted forms of compulsive behavior and/ or criminal addictive behavior.

In other words, the compulsive behavior may originally manifest in one form, while eventually, continuing in yet another form of compulsive behavior that was reproduced pursuant to one area of compulsion. For instance, avoidance and rejection can breed addiction to lying, stealing, pain, drugs, alcohol, and codependency.

Write down how you relate to this, and be very specific.

Affirmation and Meditation: "I accept God's Gift of a New Heart, Spirit, and Life in Christ for me."

"Create in me a clean heart, O God; and renew a right spirit within me" (Psalm 51:10)

STEP 3: FREEDOM FROM CONDEMNATION, GUILT, AND SHAME

STEP 3: FREEDOM FROM CONDEMNATION, GUILT, AND SHAME

One of the by-products of living in a dysfunctional family, is the development of a shame-based identity.

Shame is spawned from an emotion or feeling that "something is wrong with me".

Guilt is spawned from entertaining an emotion or feeling of "I did something wrong".

Shame has a tendency to plague an individual to be embarrassed about something that they probably (and normally) shouldn't be embarrassed about.

A common pattern of projected-shame is often experienced by individuals who have actually been "victimized" by the actions and/ or additions of others within their family of influence (wherein, another family member may be an alcoholic, drug addict, sexual offender, spiritual/ emotional abuser, or compulsive practitioner).

In such cases, the "victim" often feels shame for the action(s) of the compulsive behavior or criminal/ addictive activity of the other family member.

Toxic shame eats away at the affected individual's core moral values and even the foundation of their self-esteem, resulting in a downward spiral of despair, depression, negativity, and fatalism, pursuant to their shame-based identity.

Shame may be conveyed indirectly, as a result of the person feeling shame about another family member's addiction, actions, or problems (the "family member" could be a parent, step-parent, sibling, or another close relative).

Shame may also be conveyed pursuant to abuse, or perhaps pursuant to a failure to resolve a traumatic event that occurred (i.e., death, injury, abuse, addiction, adoption), and also, shame may be conveyed when needs and feelings haven't been properly articulated and validated within the family of origin. All of these can easily lead to a shame-based identity.

Shame may also be conveyed directly, wherein, a person is blamed for something that they were not responsible for, and thus, shame is transmitted or transferred to the person, by others (individually, or corporately within the family of influence), causing shame to linger beneath the surface of their conscious thoughts.

Ultimately, a shame-based identity causes a person to desire to hide who they are, because they associate themselves to the shame, and thus, they do not want to be known or made known, because to become visible, would allude to the unveiling of the shame that is attached to their very own identity. They have actually become the epitome of being identified with shame (within their own thoughts).

Even their own feelings can actually trigger shame. Events can trigger shame, Certain life experiences can trigger shame. The most subtle and insignificant occurrences can prove to be catastrophic bombardments of shame.

A shame-based identity can produce a codependent individual, it can also cause a person to apologize for being hurt by others. It can cause a spirit of condemnation to operate within a person's life, wherein they are easily manipulated by other family members into "working" towards being accepted, or working towards being redeemed from the shame that they often feel or experience.

Shame promotes acceptance of inferiority to other dysfunctional family members. This is, in essence, a form of codependency. Codependent person are often attracted to unhealthy, toxic relationships, wherein they are manipulated into meeting the emotional needs of others in a way that is harmful to their own spiritual and emotional health. Shame says that someone else deserves to have their needs me, but the codependent person does not.

God Himself gives us a new life that is free from condemnation, and He provides emancipation, liberation, and freedom from all guilt and even from a shame-based identity.

Write down how you relate to this, and be very specific.

Affirmation and Meditation: "I accept my New Identity in Christ Jesus."

"There is therefore now no condemnation to them which are in Christ Jesus." (Romans 8:1)

STEP 4: DELIVERED FROM PERFECTIONISM

STEP 4: DELIVERED FROM PERFECTIONISM

The Bible says, "Be perfect, therefore, as your Heavenly Father is perfect" (Matt. 5: 48), and in another place in the Bible, it says, "We... groan inwardly" (Rom. 8: 23) for the perfection and completeness that God has promised all of creation. There is something inside of all us, that desires and longs to be "complete", "whole", "lacking nothing", and/ or "perfect". This craving can be quenched and filled, solely and exclusively, by God alone. It is a yearning that is designed to bring us to Him, however, erroneously, many of us fall into the self-deception of perfectionism, as opposed to receiving the grace of God, which is available when we can acknowledge that we do not have our lives together, and that we (in and of ourselves) cannot truly attain a perfect state of being, outside of God's Presence within our lives.

There is a certain bondage to religiosity (and the deception of perfectionism), therein. It finds its roots in a false messages that brings its recipient into bondage. It is the "almost" message, the "zero-defects" message, the "hard work to cover up" message, the "idle hands" message, and the "reach-for-the-stars" message.
The "almost" message is that you "almost" did enough, but you still haven't done enough. No matter what you do, it is never enough.

The "zero-defects" message is that you can never make a mistake, and if a mistake is made, it is catastrophic and unredeemable.

The "hard work to cover up" message basically says that if you work hard enough, you can cover up your short comings.

The "idle hands" message basically says that you have to stay busy and working constantly at all times.

The "reach-for-the-stars" message is the epitome of unrealistic, unmeasurable, and unattainable goals. The Truth sets us free and makes us free.

The Truth embraces imperfection, with perfect love, which casts out all fear, anxiety, lies, imperfections, and incompleteness. The Truth makes us whole, and we are perfectly loved and received by the Truth. The Truth is a Person (and His name is Jesus Christ).

Write down how you relate to this, and be very specific.

Affirmation and Meditation: "God loves me even in my imperfection(s)."

"Come to me, all you who are weary and burdened, and I will give you rest. Take my yoke upon you and learn from me, for I am gentle and humble in heart, and you will find rest for your souls." (Matt. 11: 28-29)

STEP 5: MAKING "THE BEST" OUT OF "THE WORST"

STEP 5: MAKING "THE BEST" OUT OF "THE WORST"

By nature, most individuals have a reluctance towards bad or negative experiences. However, many of us can admit that during some of our worst experiences, we also experienced some of our most intensified-seasons of development and growth (and for many of us, it was during such times, that we learned the most about God, ourselves, and others). Sometimes, what appears to be our "worst" of times can also prove to be some of our "best" of times.

Primarily, it comes down to the power of choosing or deciding to glean from "the worst", in order to create "the best", wherein, we make "the best" out of "the worst".

Ironically, we are daily bombarded with opportunities that can catapult us into a new sphere of excellence, and in each instance, we are merely a decision away from experiencing the breakthrough that we have been praying for, coveting, and anticipating.

We all have been empowered, by God Himself, to choose or decide to: create a situation; experience (or not experience) a situation; and also, what the outcome of a situation will be.

Even in cases, where someone else originally made a decision to create a situation that directly or indirectly affected/ impacted us, the epiphany is that we are now realizing that we have the power to choose or decide what we can do about the outcome of what was initiated by someone else.

When a person reads the story of the hardships, injustices, and negative events that took place against Joseph at the hands of his own brothers, slave masters, false accusations from Potiphar's wife, and even fellow prisoners, it is amazing that Joseph is able to exercise the power to choose or decide to make the best of the worst, wherein, what had been clearly deemed as some of "the worst" scenarios imaginable becomes "the best" for Joseph.

Joseph goes as far as to choose or decide that because of all of those negative things, he is in the exact place that God's Will, Purpose, and Plan would have him to be in.

It should be emphasized that, in actuality, following all of the negativity that Joseph had been bombarded with, the summary of all of those negative experiences brought him to a place, wherein, Joseph was, at that time, the second in command in Egypt (under Pharaoh, the supreme ruler of Egypt).

Amazingly, and hopefully, we all can see that, symbolically, Pharaoh dressed Joseph in his own clothes and image, and entrusted power to Joseph to speak on the behalf of the entire kingdom as the mouthpiece of Pharaoh, in the similitude, God created us in His image, and He has entrusted power to us, to speak on the behalf of God's Kingdom, placing life and death within the power of our tongue... We can decree a thing and it will be established (because we have been made kings and priests, a royal priesthood), just as Joseph had been made a prince in Egypt (not necessarily by Pharaoh, but moreover, by God Himself).

Joseph makes peace with the past, and all of the horrible and negative experiences that we read about in Chapters 37-49 of Genesis, are summed up by Joseph's choice or decision to make the best out of the worst, *"**And Joseph said unto them, Fear not: for am I in the place of God? But as for you, ye thought evil against me; but God meant it unto good, to bring to pass, as it is this day, to save much people alive.**"* (Genesis 50: 19-20).

Admittedly (and unfortunately), many of us often use our power (or empowerment) to choose to convey that which is "negative" into that which is "negative" (and the "bad" remains "bad", and what seems to be "the worst thing that could ever happen" is forever settled as being "the worst thing that could ever happen"), because we chose or decided to make it just that, and to allow it to remain just like that.

The truth is the we are surrounded by negativity, and pursuant to our own choice, we are empowered to choose to convey that which is "negative" into that which is "positive". In other words, just like Joseph, we can take the "negative" and decree a "positive" outcome from it all.

Everything that seems to be "the worst" within our lives (whether in the past, or even at the present tense), can become "the best", if we simply choose or decide to make it "the best".

Everyone of us are aware of "negative" things that occur around us all, on a daily basis.

We should be equally-aware of the fact and truth that God has made us Peacemakers.

We are God's Agents of Change and Transition within the earth.

Today, we can identify "the negativity", "the worst", "the bad", and choose or decide to "make peace", make it "positive", make it "good", make things "right", make it "better", and make it "the best".

Write down how you can relate to this, and be very specific.

Affirmation and Meditation: "I Choose to make "the Best" out of "the Worst".

"And Joseph said unto them, Fear not: for am I in the place of God? But as for you, ye thought evil against me; but God meant it unto good, to bring to pass, as it is this day, to save much people alive." (Genesis 50:19-20)

STEP 6: THE ANSWER TO: "WHO AM I?"

STEP 6: THE ANSWER TO: "WHO AM I?"

Some of us were given a name (and/ or named) at birth, and in many cases, some of us were even named prior to our own actual birth, by someone else (a parent, guardian, or custodial individual) had already determined who we would be called or named. It is even possible, that we were told who we were (and given information about who we were to become within the family), while we were still semi-conscious of our very own existence, in our infancy.

Depending upon our cultural background, and also depending upon an individual's specific family of influence, the majority of us can relate to the fact that we were given a name and even somewhat of a family identity, before we were even aware (or conscious) of the fact that we even had a name, gender, or a family (of influence).

This, within itself, ultimately-initiated a foundational "tug-of-war" of emotional and mental "wrestling" with ourselves, with our family, and with our surroundings, over the question: "Who Am I?"

Earlier, we discussed a shamed-based identity, however, it should be noted that there are many other toxic forms of identity, that we may need to make peace with (in some form or another).

As we seek an answer to "Who Am I?', we may make decisions about our our religious pursuits, marital status, social status, our career choices, community & social justice activism, decisions about our sexuality, our gender/ sexual identity, nicknames, vocational/ professional exploits that may add certain letters to the front (or back) of our name, and other forms of name-changes, just to name a few ways and means of attempting to make peace with our past, in the area of answering "Who Am I?"

Making Peace with the Past also involves the choice of which path or paths we will choose, in order seek to define, determine and derive at the answer to: "Who Am I?" Inexhaustible-debates do not offer an "answer". We eventually choose or decide to reject or accept the truth (and even that is subject to debate about what is actually the truth). Once again, none of these debates position us to make peace with the past task of answering "Who Am I?"

The Answer to "Who Am I?" is revealed and/ or disclosed in the Word of God, and it is conveyed to our spirit, soul, mind and heart, by the Holy Spirit of Truth.

The remainder of this step shares only a "few" Biblical references to help us make peace with the past, about seeking (and finding) the answer to "Who Am I?"

Write down how you relate to this, and be very specific.

Affirmation and Meditation: "I accept God's Love for me."

"There is therefore now no condemnation to them which are in Christ Jesus." (Romans 8:1)

THE ANSWER TO: "WHO AM I?"

THE ANSWER TO: "WHO AM I?"

I am blameless and free from accusation. (Colossians 1: 22)

Christ Himself is in me. (Colossians 1: 27)

I am firmly rooted in Christ and am now being built up in Him. (Col. 2: 7)

I have been made complete in Christ. (Colossians 2: 10)

I have been spiritually circumcised. My old unregenerate nature has been removed. (Colossians 2: 11)

I have been buried, raised, and made alive with Christ. (Colossians 2: 12,13)

I died with Christ and I have been raised up with Christ. My life is now hidden with Christ in God. Christ is now my life. (Colossians 1: 1-4)

I am an expression of the life of Christ because He is my life. (Colossians 3: 4)

I am chosen of God, holy and dearly loved. (Col. 3: 12; 1 Thessalonians 1: 4)

I am a son of light and not of darkness. (1 Thessalonians 5: 5)

I have been given a spirit of power, love, and self-discipline. (2 Timothy 1: 7)

I have been saved and set apart according to God's doing. (2 Timothy 1: 9; Titus 3: 5) Because I am sanctified and am one with the Sanctifier, He is not ashamed to call me brother. (Hebrews 2: 11)

I am a holy partaker of a heavenly calling. (Hebrews 3: 1)

I have the right to come boldly before the throne of God to find mercy and grace in a time of need. (Hebrews 4: 16)

I have been born again. (1 Peter 1: 23)

I am one of God's living stones, being built up in Christ as a spiritual house. (1 Peter 2: 5)

I am a member of a chosen race, a royal priesthood, a holy nation, a people for God's own possession. (1 Peter 2: 9,10)

I am an alien and stranger to this world in which I temporarily live. (1 Peter 2: 11)

I am an enemy of the devil. (1 Peter 2: 11)

I have been given exceedingly great and precious promises by God, by which I am a partaker of God's divine nature. (2 Peter 1: 4)

I am forgiven on the account of Jesus' name. (1 John 2: 12)

I am anointed by God. (1 John 2: 27)

I am a child of God and I will resemble Christ when He returns. (1 John 3: 1,2)

I am loved. (1 John 4: 10)

I am like Christ. (1 John 4: 10)

I have life. (1 John 5: 12)

I am born of God, and the evil one... the devil... cannot touch me. (1 John 5: 8)

I have been redeemed. (Revelation 5: 9) I have been healed. (Isaiah 53: 5)

I am the salt of the earth. (Matthew 5: 13)

I am the light of the world. (Matthew 5: 14)

I am commissioned to make disciples. (Matthew 28: 19,20)

I am a child of God. (John 1: 12)

I have eternal life. (John 10: 27)

I have been given peace. (John 14: 27) I am part of the true vine, a channel of Christ's life. (John 15: 1,5)

I am clean. (John 15: 3)

I am Christ's friend. (John 15: 15)

I am chosen and appointed by Christ to bear His fruit. (John 15: 16)

I have been given glory. (John 17: 22)

I have been justified... completely forgiven and made righteous. (Romans 5: 1)

I have the right to come boldly before the throne of God to find mercy and grace in a time of need. (Hebrews 4: 16)

I have been born again. (1 Peter 1: 23)

I am one of God's living stones, being built up in Christ as a spiritual house. (1 Peter 2: 5)

I am a member of a chosen race, a royal priesthood, a holy nation, a people for God's own possession. (1 Peter 2: 9,10)

I am an alien and stranger to this world in which I temporarily live. (1 Peter 2: 11)

I am an enemy of the devil. (1 Peter 2: 11)

I have been given exceedingly great and precious promises by God by which I am a partaker of God's divine nature. (2 Peter 1: 4)

I am forgiven on the account of Jesus' name. (1 John 2: 12)

I am anointed by God. (1 John 2: 27)

I am a child of God and I will resemble Christ when He returns. (1 John 3: 1,2)

I am loved. (1 John 4: 10)

I am like Christ. (1 John 4: 10)

I have life. (1 John 5: 12)

I am the salt of the earth. (Matthew 5: 13)

I am the light of the world. (Matthew 5: 14)

I am commissioned to make disciples. (Matthew 28: 19,20)

I am a child of God. (John 1: 12)

I have eternal life. (John 10: 27)

I have been given peace. (John 14: 27)

I am part of the true vine, a channel of Christ's life. (John 15: 1,5)

I died with Christ and died to the power of sin's rule over my life.(Romans 6: 1-6)

I am a slave of righteousness. (Romans 6: 18)

I am free from sin and enslaved to God. (Romans 6: 22)

I am free forever from condemnation. (Romans 8: 1)

I am a son of God; God is spiritually my Father. (Romans 8: 14, 15; Galatians 3: 26; 4: 6)

I am a joint heir with Christ, sharing His inheritance with Him (Romans 8: 17)

I am more than a conqueror through Christ, who loves me. (Romans 8: 37)

I have faith. (Romans 12: 3)

I have been sanctified and called to holiness. (1 Corinthians 1: 2)

I have been given grace in Christ Jesus. (1Corinthians 1: 4)

I have been placed into Christ, by God's doing. (1 Corinthians 1: 30)

I have received the Spirit of God into my life that I might know the things feely given to me by God. (1 Corinthians 2: 12)

I have been given the mind of Christ. (1 Corinthians 2: 16)

I am a temple... a dwelling place... of God. His Spirit and His life dwell in me. (1 Corinthians 3: 16; 6: 19)

I am united to the Lord and am one spirit with Him. (1 Corinthians 6: 17)

I am bought with a price; I am not my own; I belong to God. (1 Corinthians 6: 19,20; 7: 23)

I am called. (1 Corinthians 7: 17)

I am a member of Christ's Body. (1 Corinthians 12: 27; Ephesians 5: 30)

I am victorious through Jesus Christ. (1 Corinthians 15: 57)

I have been established, anointed and sealed by God in Christ, and I have been given to the Holy Spirit as a pledge guaranteeing my inheritance to come. (2 Corinthians 1: 21; Ephesians 1: 13,14)

I am led by God in triumphal procession. (2 Corinthians 2: 14)

I am to God the fragrance of Christ among those who are being saved and those who are perishing. (2 Corinthians 2: 15)

I am being changed into the likeness of Christ. (2 Corinthians 3: 18)

I have died, I no longer live for myself, but for Christ. (2 Corinthians 5: 14,15)

I am a new creation. (2 Corinthians 5: 17)

I am reconciled to God and am a minister of reconciliation. (2 Corinthians 5: 18,19)

I have been made righteous. (2 Corinthians 5: 21)

I am given strength in exchange for weakness. (2 Corinthians 12: 10)

I have been crucified with Christ and it is no longer I who live, but Christ lives in me. The life I am now living is Christ's life. (Galatians 2: 20)

I am a son of God and one in Christ. (Galatians 3: 26, 28)

I am Abraham's seed... an heir of the promise. (Galatians 3: 29)

I am an heir of God since I am a son of God. (Galatians 4: 6,7)

I am a saint. (Ephesians 1: 1; ! Corinthians 1: 2; Philippians 1: 1; Colossians 1: 2)

I have been blessed with every spiritual blessing. (Ephesians 1: 3)

I was chosen in Christ before the foundation of the world to be holy and am without blame before Him. (Ephesians 1: 4)

I was predestined... determined by God... to be adopted as God's son. (Ephesians 1: 5)

I have been sealed with the Holy Spirit. (Ephesians 1: 13)

I have been made alive together with Christ. (Ephesians 2: 5)

I have been raised up and seated with Christ in heaven. (Ephesians 2: 6)

I am God's workmanship... His handiwork... born anew in Christ to do His work. (Ephesians 2: 10) I have direct access to God through the Spirit. (Ephesians 2: 18)

I am a fellow citizen with the rest of God's family. (Ephesians 2: 19)

I may approach God with boldness, freedom, and confidence. (Ephesians 3: 12)

I am righteous and holy. (Ephesians 2: 24)

I am a citizen of heaven, seated in heaven right now. (Philippians 3: 20; Ephesians 2: 6)
I am capable. (Philippians 4: 13)
I have been rescued from the domain of Satan's rule and transferred to the kingdom of Christ. (Colossians 1: 13)
I have been redeemed and forgiven of all my sins. The debt against me has been cancelled. (Colossians 1: 14)

STEP 7: FORGIVING: PEACEMAKING 101

STEP 7: FORGIVING: PEACEMAKING 101

The Biblical definition of "forgiving" is synonymous with "peacemaking".

"Forgiving" and "Peacemaking" is all about reconciling offenses, blotting out transgressions, disregarding trespasses, deleting formally-retained or harbored bitterness, releasing resentment, and pardoning wrong-doing(s).

For many, forgiving is the doorway to peacemaking, but, we seldom have a desire to walk through such a door. However, peacemaking is virtually impossible, wherein, forgiving has been avoided and/ or evaded.

Upon true examination, peacemaking will begin to be personally made manifest, and realized, when we acknowledge our need to address the issue of forgiving others, our society, ourselves, and even our God (primarily, because we have been harboring unforgiveness within our heart against God, ourselves, our family of influence, our society, and others).

For many of us, our social environment (and/ or society) has historically scorned us, with seemingly-irreparable injury, and we must choose or make a decision to make peace with a past, that is presently-impacting our present society.

The application of this decision is inexhaustible, and it can be applied to everything from Adam and Eve, to Hitler, to globalized-monopolies, and innumerable environmental, economical and social justice issues that have caused degrees of injury.

The general concept is that there are things that we cannot control within our society, that we need to make peace with, if we are going to overcome (keep in mind, our section on the biblical definition of a Peacemaker, and what it biblically means to make peace).

Obviously, many of us need to forgive others, as an essential step towards making peace with the past, however, many of us also need to begin to forgive ourselves, and even God, because our very own resentment towards ourselves and God has been a major hindrance to us experiencing the peace that we have been pursuing.

Imagine your life, void of offenses, transgression, trespasses, wrong-doing, and injustices... A life where everything negative has been removed, blotted out, reconciled, and forgiven... That, my friend, is what life is like when you make peace with your past...

Forgiving is form of Reconciling, and Reconciling is a form of Peacemaking...

Write down how you relate to this, and be very specific.

Affirmation and Meditation: "I make, experience, and enjoy peace."

"For if ye forgive men their trespasses, your heavenly Father will also forgive you: But if ye forgive not men their trespasses, neither will your Father forgive your trespasses." (Matthew 6: 14-15)

STEP 8: THE "BLESSING" REVEALED: YOUR PAST, PRESENT, AND FUTURE

STEP 8: THE "BLESSING" REVEALED: YOUR PAST, PRESENT, AND FUTURE

The "*past*" is a "blessing", and everything that has taken place in your "past" is a "blessing", in one way or in another. You should be extremely excited to acknowledge the fact that no matter what has (or hasn't) transpired within your past (including pain and numbness), everything that has happened has led you right to the exact place that you are in right now, at this very moment, reading this book, and taking charge of making peace with your past!

Your examination, evaluation, and perception (in reference to your past), has the kinetic power to usher you into a sphere of the spectacular and supernatural (wherein, lies an atrium to phenomenal new beginnings, with multi-faceted, and multi-leveled experiences of healing, reconciliation, and victory)!

The "*presen*t" (of your "today" and "now") is a "blessing", and that is one of the reasons that we refer to it as "the present", because in all actuality, it is a "present" (or a "gift") from God Himself.

You should be extra grateful to discern the inexhaustible possibilities that you have been "gifted", pursuant to your present state of being, for within your "today" and "now", are the time-imposed trajectory choices, which hold the keys to addressing the doors of your past and future (wherein, you can choose to open or close doors, at your own will... right now... concerning your past and your future!

The "*future*" is a "blessing", especially for you, because you are reading this book, and actually embarking upon making peace with your past!

You are the agent of your own expectation(s), creating and cultivating your own anticipations, opportunities, realities, legacy, longevity, destiny/ destination, and expected "ending(s)", as well as perpetual "beginning( )" of renewed goals and accomplishments (which can be renewed, on a daily basis), in accordance to your own faith (and/or belief system)!

Write down how you relate to this, and be very specific.

Affirmation and Meditation: "I am blessed (by my past, present, and future)!"

"Therefore if any man be in Christ, he is a new creature: old things are passed away; behold, all things are become new. And all things are of God," (2 Corinthians 5: 17-18a)

STEP 9: RE-DEFINING AND EXPERIENCING "J.O.Y."

STEP 9: RE-DEFINING AND EXPERIENCING "J.O.Y."

By nature, we all have certain things that constitute our personal definition of joy, and within that definition is also the composition of how we personally experience of our self-defined sense of joy.

The reality and relativity of our existence and co-existence is a factor that we cannot afford to ignore, neglect, nor reject, because we are relational, by creation. We may have chosen to reject **Jesus** (and/ or the existence of God), not realizing that our choice and rejection (within itself) actually confirms and validates His existence.

Likewise, we can ignore or reject **others** and even our need for others, but once again, our action, alludes to our actual need for others.

Furthermore, even if (or when) you may have been neglectful in defining and recognizing the value, self-worth, purposeful significance that resonates within **yourself**, you are actually of great import.

A critical component to making peace is being reconciled within the totality of our life, surrounding environment, society, and/ or creation as we know it, which simplistically alludes to how we perceive ourselves, others, and the universe/ creation.

Your definition of joy, may need to be redefined, in order for you to truly experience it. The truth is that the foundation of joy, must be considered as the following, and built upon this new-found "reality"... I offer the following acronym to help you to redefine and experience joy... **J.O.Y. (Jesus Others Yourself)**...

The manner in which you define/ re-define each of these, will assuredly prove to be a factor in you actually making peace with your past. How you relate to God, Others, and Yourself is essential. Begin to re-define **"J.O.Y."**, by beginning to write a renewed definition beside each one that will allude to you experiencing **"joy"**:

Jesus:

Others:

Yourself:

Write down how you relate to this, and be very specific.

Affirmation and Meditation: "I embrace **J.O.Y.!**"

"These things have I spoken unto you, that my joy might remain in you, and that your joy might be full." (John 15: 11)

STEP 10: PURPOSE AND VISION: BALANCE AND RESILIENCE

STEP 10: PURPOSE AND VISION: BALANCE AND RESILIENCE

PURPOSE: Making peace with your past will require **purpose**. God operates with purpose, and as a child of God, we have been given a ministry of reconciliation (a ministry of making peace), and we are commissioned to embrace our purpose, and also to walk therein. There is a divine purpose that is nestled within your past experiences (" and to everything, there is a season and purpose"). Likewise, there is a time for the purpose to be disclosed, realized, and unveiled, wherein, we can decide to begin to accept our purpose, in order to live, move, and have our being, in the full manifestation of our purpose.

"To every thing there is a season, and a time to every **purpose** under the heaven:" (Ecclesiastes 3: 1) "

But rise, and stand upon thy feet: for I have appeared unto thee for this **purpose**, to make thee a minister and a witness both of these things which thou hast seen, and of those things in the which I will appear unto thee;" (Acts 26: 16)

"And we know that all things work together for good to them that love God, to them who are the called according to his **purpose**." (Romans 8: 28)

VISION: Making peace with your past will require **vision**. If you cannot envision "making peace", you will never truly experience it. The lack of a vision assures failure, along with perishing in a sphere that is void of peace (keep in mind, that there is no peace for the wicked). However, peace abounds in the presence of God. Peacemaking is the essence of all of God's creation, for we witness within the Word of God, that the peacemaking Lamb of God was already "slain" prior to the foundation of the world, indicating that making peace was at the heart and vision of God, in creation itself. We are called to embody and personify the vision of God, in Christ Jesus.

BALANCE: Making peace with your past will require **balance**. We often suffer from extremism, heightened by our decision to decline to properly (and positively) prioritize. Discernment is deciding to balance the process of making peace.

RESILIENCE: Making peace with your past will require **resilience**. Resilience is synonymous to resurrection, reconciliation, and restoration. The ability to rise from the embers of what was destroyed, even where the offense once abounded, we can find the resiliency of peacemaking.

Write down how you relate to this, and be very specific.

Affirmation and Meditation: "I am making peace with my past."

"Brethren, I count not myself to have apprehended: but this one thing I do, forgetting those things which are behind, and reaching forth unto things which are before," (Philippians 3: 13)

STEP 11: THE EMPOWERMENT OF "I CAN"

STEP 11: THE EMPOWERMENT OF "I CAN"

"And the Lord said unto Moses, See, I have made thee a god to Pharaoh: and Aaron thy brother shall be thy prophet. Thou shalt speak all that I command thee: and Aaron thy brother shall speak unto Pharaoh, that he send the children of Israel out of his land. And I will harden Pharaoh's heart, and multiply my signs and my wonders in the land of Egypt." (Exodus 7: 1-3)

In Exodus 7: 1-3, God told Moses that he would make Moses to be like a god to Pharaoh, and also, that Aaron (Moses' brother) would be like Moses' own prophet. This truth was spoken into Moses' spirit, and by grace, Moses was enabled and/ or empowered to believe what God said to him. I share this in the context of the reality that Moses did, in all actuality, wrestle with certain things that God had shared with him, as many of us do as well. Moses not only struggled with believing God, but he also struggled with believing in himself. In any event, we see that the finality of it, was that Moses was able to believe God, and to believe in the God-given spirit of faith that had been imparted unto Moses to believe in himself, and in God. Scripture bears witness to a transfer of the spirit that was upon Moses, onto other individuals, who would share in the work of making peace or bringing people to a "place of peace", when disputes or issues arose amongst them (Exodus 18: 13-26, v. 23 "place of peace"). All of this points to the fact that God desires us to freely receive from Him, in order to freely give to others. We receive peace, in order to impart peace. God gives us the authority, power, and keys of the kingdom to decree a thing and it is established (because He has made us priests and kings). God is God. God created (and re-creates) us in His Divine Nature (in Christ). God speaks, and it is so, according to whatever He speaks. Likewise, God empowers you and I with the empowerment of "I Can".

There is a key that is at the heart of making peace with the past, and that is the power your belief system. To the individual who believes that all things are possible, nothing is impossible to the person who actually believes. The empowerment of "I Can" turns dreams into realities.

Your focus, your determination, your "I Know", and your "I Can" is omnipotent (all-powerful and/ or all-empowering) by Divine-Design. When it comes to either negativity or positivity (and/ or both), your focus has the final say-so. By focusing upon what you do not have, you do not have. By focusing upon what you cannot do, you cannot do whatever it (or that) is. In many instances, we underestimate the power of our own unbelief, wherein, our own unbelief has a tendency to "trump" our professed belief. God and His creation groans, as he awaits the process of reconciliation and making peace. It is highly probable that we, like God, are groaning, pursuant to the results of what we have created with our own words (of both, belief and unbelief).

When we harness the power of "I Know", "I Will", "I Am", and "I Can", we unleash the energy of the universe into whatever we target (or focus) our "I Can" upon, at that given moment.

Write down how you relate to this, and be very specific.

Affirmation and Meditation: "I can make peace with my past."

"I can do all things through Christ which strengtheneth me." (Philippians 4:13)

STEP 12: APPLICATION: The Empowerment of "I Can"
(I Can, I Will, I Have, I Have Learned)

STEP 12: APPLICATION: The Empowerment of "I Can" (I Can, I Will, I Have, I Have Learned)

This unit is unique, in that, **YOU** are the co-author of this unit...

God, the Holy Spirit (within you), is the Author, and if you are willing to come into agreement with God, His Word and/ or with the Word of God, you receive the power to "co-author" your new life (in every area that you choose to apply it)!

Life and death is in the power of your tongue, and you have been given the authority (in Christ Jesus), to decree a thing, and it shall be established unto you! Whatsoever you sow or speak, or write, you will receive, according to your faith!

With that much briefly stated, this unit will become a catalyst that will govern the trajectory of your own life, pursuant to your own choices and decisions...

Your assignment, therefore, is to experience the empowerment of "I Can" in your own following statements:

I CAN...

I WILL...

I HAVE...

I HAVE LEARNED...

CONCLUSION: "MAKING PEACE WITH YOUR PAST" (REFLECTION AND APPLICATION)

CONCLUSION: "MAKING PEACE WITH YOUR PAST" (REFLECTION AND APPLICATION)

Your mind is a phenomenal "power tool" that creates your reality (consciously and unconsciously).

Everything that you think about, is creating your world. When you begin to exercise the power tool of your mind to visualize peace, you can actualize and realize peace.

Your senses are connected to your mindset, and thus, your senses align with your mind. When your mind is troubled, your senses align with your troubled mind, and often this is the atrium to multi-faceted health issues (including mental health issues).

This reality can spill over into your financial health and into the health of your relationships (wherein, they become healthy or unhealthy relationships).

When your mind is uneasy, discomforted, unsettled, and void of peace, it affects the health of your mind (your choices, decisions, discernment, etc.).

Unhealthy relationships are birthed (and/ or continue); unhealthy financial decisions persist; unhealthy choices in dietary issues abound; an unhealthy mind creates an unhealthy environment for itself (ultimately, an unhealthy life of multi-faceted, self-sabotage).

Peace is a state of mind. Your mind can be at peace, even in the midst of calamity, chaos, destruction, pestilence, and the tempestuous storms of life.

I have personally witnessed individuals spend an entire measurable year, in willful unforgiveness, resentment, bitterness, gossip, festering and spreading lies, and ultimately being an agent of discord.

For some, it's been years (seemingly, even a lifetime), wherein such a state has existed (and continued) in their lives.

The Truth (Jesus Christ/ The Word of God) comes to set them free from the destruction of erroneous thinking patterns (Psalm 107: 20), but they still **_choose_** bondage, slavery, wilderness-wandering, as opposed to **_choosing_** to enter into the Promised Land of God (wherein, all of the promises are "Yes" and "Amen", when we put them into practice).

Do you want to be **made whole**?

Do you want to be **healed**?

Do you want to be **set free** from your painful past?

Do you want to make peace with your past? What do you really want? In spite of what your own mouth may say in response to this inquiry, **your actions will actually determine your true answer**.

"Making Peace With Your Past" is your **duty** to God, yourself, your family of influence, and your community.

"**Owe** no man nothing, but to **love** him".

Your "**debt**" to God and society is to enlist as a **peacemaker** within the kingdom of God.

The universe has been groaning and awaiting you…

"Blessed are the peacemakers: for they shall be called the children of God." (Matthew 5: 9)

EPILOGUE

In my youth, my life was traumatically-impacted, by a confrontational event that served as a spiritual "beckoning", from God Himself to my spirit... That activating-event of undeniable "accountability" was the Sunday that I sat on the front pew of Greater Ward A.M.E. Church, as my cousin, Marvin D. Cloud (now, Rev. Marvin D. Cloud) preached his first sermon...Over the years, there is no way to truly vocalize how God used that event in my life to "prick" at my heart...

As time progressed, Marvin shared a vision with my parents, our church, and with many others, in reference to something that the Lord had placed upon his heart (which could be deemed as to a facet of ministry outreach), and my parents were more than honored to "sow a seed" into his ministry vision, which, in part, became known as the Gospel Monthly Magazine (GMM)...

I recall my parents encouraging me to prayerfully-consider submitting some of my writings to Marvin, to see if he wanted to include any of them as a potential corner article in the GMM...

The truth is that I actually began teaching Sunday School at the age of 8, and I was officially placed on the roster as a Sunday School teacher at the age of 12. As a Sunday School teacher, I wrote numerous articles, however, I never submitted any of them to Marvin...

...Disobedience has its cost...Years later, while housed on the TDCJ McConnell Unit in Beeville, Tx. (with a Life Sentence, along with a consecutive Thirty Year Sentence), I would receive a monthly subscription of the GMM (which was somewhat of a monthly "reminder", from God Himself, that I still needed to submit my writings to Marvin)... Decades passed...

In the Lord's Divine Timing, I wholeheartedly submitted to God's Will, Purpose, and Plan for my life of ministry, and I began the process of making peace with my past, to the extent that I even began to facilitate weekly Bible Studies under the umbrella of the TDCJ Chaplaincy Department (on a developing subject matter of Making Peace With Your Past).

I personally witnessed individuals (within those weekly small group classes) make peace with their past, pursuant to the power of God in Christ Jesus!
After serving twenty-three years in TDCJ, the Lord allowed me to be miraculously-released on parole, wherein, I was blessed to facilitate bi-weekly, faith-based recovery classes (about Making Peace With Your Past), within recovery centers, various community centers, TDCJ State Jails, Youth Offender Programs, and TDCJ Prison Units. It has taken me 40 years to finally "submit" to writing and publishing this book...

May this small act of **_obedience_** be honored by God... I love you, Rev. Marvin D. Cloud ("Cuz")...

I am so thankful for your obedience... As you have followed Christ, I now follow and obey Him as well... I am at peace with God, and with the totality of my past... My "past" now includes, my **_obedient_** submission to God's Will, Purpose, and Plan for my life and ministry...

My prayer for you (as the reader, hearer, and doer), is that this will be your season to begin *"Making Peace With Your Past"*..."

-Master Feldon Bonner II

"Blessed are the peacemakers, for they shall be called the children of God." (Matt. 5: 9)

MAKING PEACE WITH YOUR PAST: A 12 STEP GUIDE TO A PEACEFULLY PRODUCTIVE LIFE

by Feldon Bonner II

(Foreword by Ivan Sanchez)

www.ingramcontent.com/pod-product-compliance
Lightning Source LLC
LaVergne TN
LVHW091225080426
835509LV00009B/1170